THE GIFT OF CHRISTMAS

Other Crossway Books by R. Kent Hughes

Abba Father

Disciplines of a Godly Man

Set Apart

PREACHING THE WORD SERIES

The Sermon on the Mount: The Message of the Kingdom

Mark: Jesus, Servant and Savior, Volumes 1 and 2

Luke: That You May Know the Truth, Volumes 1 and 2

John: That You May Believe

Acts: The Church Afire

Romans: Righteousness from Heaven

Ephesians: The Mystery of the Body of Christ

Colossians and Philemon: The Supremacy of Christ

1 and 2 Timothy: To Guard the Deposit
(coauthored with Bryan Chapell)

Hebrews: An Anchor for the Soul, Volumes 1 and 2

James: Faith That Works

The Gift of Christmas

R. Kent Hughes

CROSSWAY

A DIVISION OF GOOD NEWS PUBLISHERS

The Gift of Christmas

Revised edition (original title *The Gift*), copyright © 2003 by R. Kent Hughes.

Original edition copyright © 1994 by R. Kent Hughes.

Published by Crossway Books
a division of Good News Publishers
1300 Crescent Street
Wheaton, Illinois 60187

Cover design: Robin Black, UDG | DesignWorks, www.designworks.com
Cover and interior photos: SuperStock, Inc.

First printing, original edition, 1994
First printing, revised edition, new title, 2003

Printed in Italy

All Scripture quotations are taken from *The Holy Bible: English Standard Version,* copyright © 2001 by Crossway Bibles, a division of Good News Publishers. Used by permission. All rights reserved.

Library of Congress Cataloging-in-Publication Data

Hughes, R. Kent.
    The gift of Christmas / R. Kent Hughes.—Rev. ed.
       p. cm.
Rev. ed. of: The Gift. 1994.
    ISBN 1-58134-530-5 (alk. paper)
    1. Jesus Christ--Nativity. 2. Christian biography—Palestine.
I. Hughes, R. Kent. Gift. II. Title.
    BT315.3.H84 2003
    232.92--dc21

              2003007129

PBI	10	09	08	07	06	05	04	03
10	09	08	07	06	05	04	03	02	01

My deepest appreciation to Dr. Lane T. Dennis,

president of Crossway Books, who conceived

this project, and whose commitment to excellence in publishing

made this book possible.

CONTENTS

THE ANNUNCIATION OF JOHN

LUKE 1:5-25

With a haunting metaphor, the Gospel of Luke describes Jesus' birth as "the sunrise . . . from on high" (1:78). The night before that sunrise had indeed been long and bleak. For four hundred years there had been no word of prophecy, no break in the darkness, no sign of the Son.

Where was the "sun of righteousness" prophesied by Malachi who would "rise with healing in its wings" (4:2)? And where was the one who would come first to "prepare the way of the Lord" (Isaiah 40:3)? Now the long darkness was about to end. The great plans of God Almighty, laid in eternal ages past, would begin to unfold as angels rushed to set the stage for the coming dawn.

A gracious gift would come from her barren womb.

The opening scene would be in the Temple, which housed the heartbeat of Jewish faith. It was here that the curtain would begin to rise on the eternal drama.

Who would the leading players be? Unlikely by human standards, it was an elderly couple—Zechariah and Elizabeth by name—who had been cast for two major parts. Who were these two "unknowns" chosen for so great a role in the drama of the ages?

Zechariah was an ordinary country priest. His wife Elizabeth could trace her own priestly lineage back to Aaron. "Both," the Bible tells us, were "righteous before God, walking blamelessly in all the commandments and statutes of the Lord. But they had no child, because Elizabeth was barren, and both were advanced in years."

Like other childless couples at any time in history, Elizabeth and Zechariah knew the aching disappointment of being childless. But in the ancient biblical world, the pain was multiplied, for barrenness was considered a disgrace and even a punishment.

The years must have taken away all hope. The spotted, worn hands of this righteous couple would never hold a child of their own.

Elizabeth and Zechariah did not know, however, that the dawn was about to break. The occasion came on one of the two weeks each year that Zechariah was appointed to serve in the Temple. And now, chosen by an elaborate process of drawing lots, he had the added honor of offering incense in the Holy of Holies. In an instant he was at the apex of his life! Oh, if Elizabeth could see this! What a joy he would have in telling her.

As the evening fell, the great moment approached. Zechariah stood in the heart of the gleaming Temple. Outside in the Temple courtyard the faithful worshipers were praying.

Zechariah stepped into the Holy of Holies. Before him rose the richly embroidered curtain, resplendent with cherubim woven in scarlet, blue, purple, and gold. To his left stood the table of showbread. Immediately in front of him was the golden altar of incense. To his right burned the golden candlestick. Zechariah purified the altar and waited joyously for the signal. He poured the incense on the white-hot coals, and the sacrifices went up to God, wrapped in a mixture of sweet incense and believing prayer.

Zechariah's heart soared with the curling fragrance, but suddenly his heart spasmed in divine arrest! For before him, at the right side of the incense altar, stood an angel of the Lord. Gripped with fear, Zechariah's heart began to race. Astoundingly, the angel was none other than Gabriel himself, who had last appeared five hundred years before to the prophet Daniel.

Stricken with fear, the angel comforted Zechariah. "Do not be afraid," the angel said, "for your prayer has been heard." What prayer had been heard? Most likely it was Zechariah's priestly prayer for the redemption of Israel. Little did he know that the child he and Elizabeth would have would be the dawn of the answer! As Gabriel spoke, the long night of prophetic silence came to an end. After four hundred years without a word, Gabriel broke the silence with the stunning news that the messianic age was about to begin.

What was this message, borne from the presence of God Himself on angel's wings to an ordinary country priest? Gabriel's opening line astounded Zechariah. "Your wife Elizabeth will bear you a son, and you shall call his name John." The name John means "God has been gracious," and the logic of the name was clear. Zechariah had just prayed for God's grace to be poured out on the nation of Israel—and his prayer had been heard. A son would be born whose very name was "God has been gracious." Aged Elizabeth would experience a maternal spring; a gracious gift would come from her barren womb.

Do not
be afraid,
for your
prayer
has been
heard.

As the awesome presence of Gabriel would suggest, this would be no ordinary son: "You will have joy and gladness, and many will rejoice at his birth, for he will be great before the Lord . . . he will turn many of the children of Israel to the Lord their God, and he will go before him in the spirit and power of Elijah, to turn the hearts of the fathers to the children, and the disobedient to the wisdom of the just, to make ready for the Lord a people prepared." Their son would be none other than the one prophesied by Isaiah to "prepare the way of the LORD"—the coming Messiah.

You will have joy and gladness, and many will rejoice at his birth, for he will be great before the Lord . . .

The world stopped, and Gabriel was silent. Zechariah spoke: "How shall I know this?" he asked in woeful disbelief. "I am an old man, and my wife is advanced in years."

How could he not believe! He knew the Scriptures. He knew of God's divine intervention in the births of Isaac and Samson and Samuel. He was a priest, a man of God, known for his piety and faith. He was in the very Temple of God, the Holy of Holies, and before him stood the awesome angel of the Lord.

Yet Zechariah disbelieved! Gabriel's rebuke was swift:

I am Gabriel, who stands in the presence of God, and I was sent to speak to you and to bring you this good news. And behold, you will be silent and unable to speak until the day that these things take place, because you did not believe my words, which will be fulfilled in their time.

Zechariah's penalty fit the offense. His tongue, unwilling to confess belief, was struck speechless. What torture! He had so much to tell dear Elizabeth. It seemed impossible to communicate what had happened, but somehow he succeeded.

And then Elizabeth conceived! Her old body assumed the health of maternal bloom, and they were out of their minds with excitement. Elizabeth expressed it this way: "Thus the Lord has done for me in the days when he looked on me, to take away my reproach among people."

The Sun would not rise until the birth of Jesus, but a pre-dawn glow had appeared on the horizon. In six months Elizabeth and Zechariah would host the young mother-to-be of the Son of God. They would hear Mary sing the *Magnificat,* and speechless Zechariah would one day sing his song of faith, the *Benedictus.*

For Elizabeth and Zechariah, as we see them in Luke 1, the "sunrise . . . from on high" had not yet come, but for us, He has. The pre-dawn glow prophesied by Gabriel has become full day. Jesus Himself later said, "I am the light of the world. Whoever follows me will not walk in darkness, but will have the light of life" (John 8:12).

THE ANNUNCIATION OF JESUS

LUKE 1:26-38

The annunciation story is a story of singular beauty and wonder. But its beauty is especially piercing because it is true, firmly fixed in real people in an actual place in history.

The setting was in fact a shock to first-century Jews—that the angel Gabriel would ignore Judea, the heartland of God's work through the centuries, and go instead to the region of Galilee, a land of abiding contempt because of its religious impurity. Even more, that the angel would bypass the majestic city of Jerusalem for the lowly village of Nazareth.

Nazareth was a "non-place"—not even mentioned in the Old Testament or in any Jewish writings of the day. Nazareth was a shoddy, corrupt halfway stop between the port cities of Tyre and Sidon, overrun by Gentiles and Roman soldiers. Straight-talking Nathaniel, Jesus' disciple, even exclaimed, "Can anything good come out of Nazareth?" (John 1:46). Everybody knew Nazareth wasn't much.

He will be great and will be called the Son of the Most High.

Yet Gabriel skipped Judea and Jerusalem and even the Jewish Temple, the most holy place of all. By what strange, divine design would the choice fall upon the humble home of Mary, which certainly wasn't much?

And in the world's eyes, Mary surely wasn't much either. She was too young to have accomplished anything—perhaps fourteen, more probably just twelve, as leading scholars conclude. A poor peasant girl, in a no-place village, she would have been illiterate, her knowledge of the Scriptures limited to what she had heard in the synagogue and committed to memory in her home.

We can only imagine how Mary felt when Gabriel appeared to her. In the familiarity of Luke's words we almost miss the startling reality:

> *In the sixth month the angel Gabriel was sent from God to a city of Galilee named Nazareth, to a virgin betrothed to a man whose name was Joseph, of the house of David. And the virgin's name was Mary. And he came to her and said, "Greetings, O favored one, the Lord is with you!"*

What could Mary have thought—the angel Gabriel standing before her, and then this strange greeting? What could it possibly mean?

We must all agree that the Virgin Mary is the most blessed of women, and that "the Blessed Virgin Mary" is therefore a fitting designation. The title springs naturally from Mary's own words in her *Magnificat*: "From now on all generations will call me blessed" (Luke 1:48). Mary was the only woman out of all the billions ever to live on our planet who was chosen to carry and nurse God's Son. For that we must call her "blessed." The Savior would come from her womb. He bore the look of her human features. Jesus' face could be seen in hers.

Mary's response to Gabriel's greeting reveals another of her blessed heart's qualities: She "was greatly troubled at the saying, and tried to discern what kind of greeting this might be." Literally, she kept pondering the meaning of the greeting, searching its depths.

This is a truly remarkable picture. Young and inexperienced as she was, Mary was reflective and meditative. She knew the theological grace of contemplation. She stood atop the mount of grace and meditated upon what this meant *for* her and what it would require *from* her. In our frenetic, uncontemplative age, Mary's example has special relevance. For only those who take the time to ponder God's Word will experience the birth of the Savior in their lives.

If Mary was surprised by the initial greeting, how much more by the Annunciation itself! Gabriel's words are shocking: "And the angel said to her, 'Do not be afraid, Mary, you have found favor with God. And behold, you will conceive in your womb and bear a son, and you shall call his name Jesus.'"

At this point Mary hardly could have understood everything. "Jesus" was a common name that meant "savior." But what did this really mean? "He will be great and will be called the Son of the Most High," Gabriel continued—and the vagueness immediately evaporated.

The impact must have been staggering. The child would be God's own Son: "And the Lord God will give to him the throne of his father David, and he will reign over the house of Jacob forever, and of his kingdom there

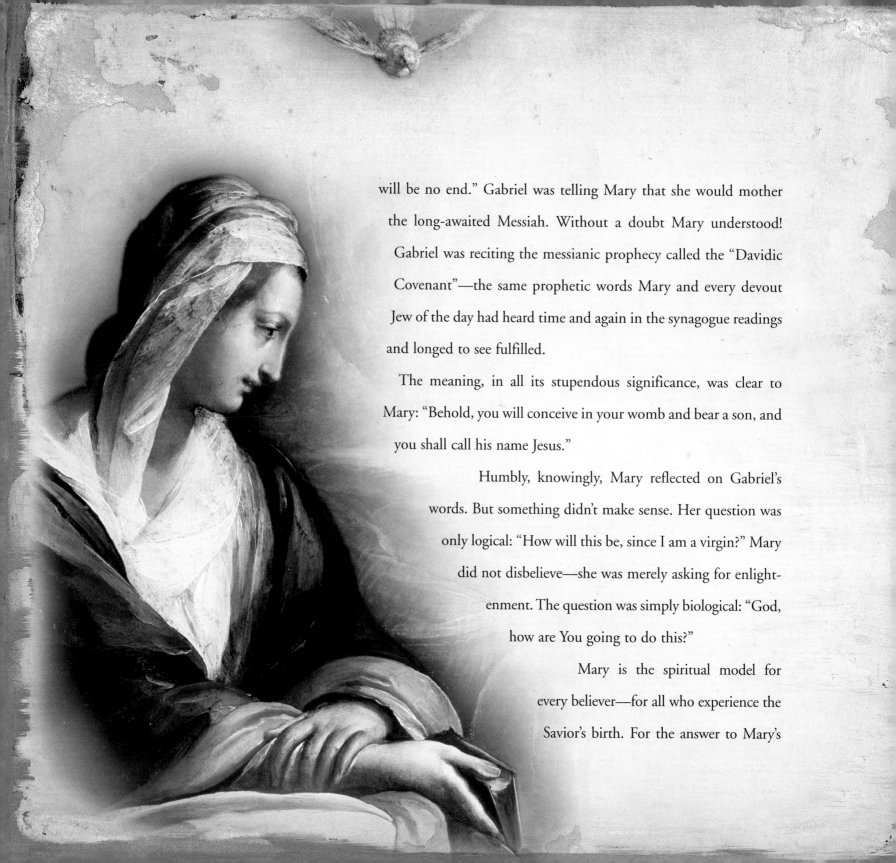

will be no end." Gabriel was telling Mary that she would mother the long-awaited Messiah. Without a doubt Mary understood! Gabriel was reciting the messianic prophecy called the "Davidic Covenant"—the same prophetic words Mary and every devout Jew of the day had heard time and again in the synagogue readings and longed to see fulfilled.

The meaning, in all its stupendous significance, was clear to Mary: "Behold, you will conceive in your womb and bear a son, and you shall call his name Jesus."

Humbly, knowingly, Mary reflected on Gabriel's words. But something didn't make sense. Her question was only logical: "How will this be, since I am a virgin?" Mary did not disbelieve—she was merely asking for enlightenment. The question was simply biological: "God, how are You going to do this?"

Mary is the spiritual model for every believer—for all who experience the Savior's birth. For the answer to Mary's question—"God, how is it possible?"—must be found by everyone who would have the birth of the Savior in their own lives.

The answer Mary received marvelously foreshadowed God's personal answer to us. "The Holy Spirit will come upon you," Gabriel explained, "and the power of the Most High will overshadow you; therefore the child to be born will be called holy—the Son of God." The words of Gabriel describe nothing less than the virgin birth of Christ.

God's answer to Mary beautifully parallels the experience of all who have personally come to know the birth of Christ as the miraculous, life-giving work of the Holy Spirit come upon them, transforming them and bestowing life within.

Mary's encounter with Gabriel was nearly over, but before returning to the heavens, Gabriel left Mary with a sign and an unshakable promise. "And behold, your relative Elizabeth in her old age has also conceived a son, and this is the sixth month with her who was called barren." All of this is incredibly impossible, the

THEREFORE THE CHILD TO BE BORN WILL BE CALLED HOLY— THE SON OF GOD.

modern critic would say. And as if to answer directly, Gabriel proclaimed the timeless truth that "nothing will be impossible with God." God will fulfill His Word. It is as simple as that.

Mary, of course, knew instinctively that her story would be questioned, and indeed even Joseph himself doubted. She knew that the death penalty was prescribed for adultery in ancient Israel. But despite these daunting realities, Mary's ringing response was, "Behold, I am the servant of the Lord; let it be to me according to your word." Mary's submission to God was total and absolute.

And to all who will humbly come to Him in belief, He gives the gift of eternal life.

For Luke the theologian, Mary was the model for all who experience the birth of Christ in their lives. The answer to all our deepest needs comes in one word: *submission* to God's will. "I am the servant of the Lord; let it be to me according to your word." These are the words that bring God's blessing. These are the words that bring eternal life.

In the world's eyes, Mary certainly wasn't much—a poor peasant girl in a no-place village. But she was willing to submit herself completely to the Lord. As such she reveals the eternal truth that God comes only to those who are humble and poor in spirit, who acknowledge their weakness and sin, who realize they need Him—they cannot make it on their own. And to all who humbly come to Him in belief, He gives the gift of eternal life.

The Visitation

L U K E   1 : 3 9 - 5 6

The angel Gabriel's annunciation declared the astounding facts of the Incarnation; the Virgin Mary's response revealed an astonishing heart. Her young heart showcased the essential characteristics of all who would experience the birth of Christ in their lives. There was her *humility,* as she was deeply conscious of her spiritual need. There was her *contemplative* soul, as she thought deeply on spiritual matters. She was profoundly *believing,* as she wondered at the miracle of her virgin conception. She was sweetly *submissive,* yielding completely to God's will. She was indeed "blessed," a living model for those who would know the life of Christ in their hearts.

What further astounds us is her tender age. As was the custom after betrothal, the bride would live with her family for a year before formally moving to the groom's home. Mary was just beyond puberty and probably hadn't even attained her full height and figure. Though it may offend the modern mind, a twelve- or thirteen-year-old girl was chosen not only to be the virgin mother of our Lord, but also to be a model of sublime faith that has challenged the greatest of saints.

We take up Mary's story with her immediate decision to visit her aged, barren relative Elizabeth. Luke reports Mary's decision with the matter-of-fact words, "In those days Mary arose and went with haste into the hill country, to a town in Judah." Gabriel had just revealed to Mary that Elizabeth was pregnant and six months along. Her pregnancy was miraculous, but we must never confuse how vastly different it was from the miracle in Mary. Barren Elizabeth was not a virgin, and Zechariah was the natural father of her child. But what a surge of joy swept through Mary as she heard the shocking good news about the miracle in Elizabeth's womb, for it bore parallel testimony to God's power.

Mary made hasty arrangements with her parents (did she tell them? we do not know) and rushed the eighty to one hundred miles south, a three- or four-day journey, to the countryside of Judea. She couldn't wait to get there. She and Elizabeth were both in miraculous pregnancies! And then she was there, unannounced, silhouetted in the old couple's doorway.

There was primal human joy in the meeting of these two expectant mothers—one in the flower of youth, the other's bloom long gone. These two were to become innocent co-conspirators, soul-sisters in the divine plan to save the lost.

The meeting was appropriately dramatic. Luke records that Mary "entered the house of Zechariah and greeted Elizabeth. And when Elizabeth heard the greeting of Mary, the baby leaped in her womb." Remarkably, the unborn baby John responded even before Elizabeth had a chance to answer Mary. In startled wonder Elizabeth replied, "Behold, when the sound of your greeting came to my ears, the baby in my womb leaped for joy."

Only a mother can relate to the sensation here described. It was more than a prenatal kick or turn, but a leap, an upward vault. The same word, in fact, is used to describe skipping or leaping like that of a sheep in the field.

Why did Elizabeth's baby soar? The answer is twofold. First, she carried a prophet in her womb, and this was his first prophecy. John the Baptist's prophetic ministry was beginning three months before his birth. The Holy Spirit, already filling the unborn child, prompted his inner vault.

Second, John leaped because he was overcome with the emotion of joy. The exact meaning is that he "leaped with delight." What an amazing fact! John was but a six-month-old fetus, and yet he experienced emotion, joyous delight. Here is incontrovertible testimony to the pre-birth personhood of John the Baptist. John was about nine inches long and weighed about one and a half pounds. He looked like a perfect miniature newborn. His skin was translucent. He had fingerprints and toe-prints. Sometimes he opened his eyes for brief periods and gazed into the liquid darkness of the womb.

As John vaulted in his mother's womb, Elizabeth too underwent an elevation of soul. The prophetic Spirit seized her, and she saluted Mary as the mother of the Lord. With a great shout she exclaimed, "Blessed are you among women, and blessed is the fruit of your womb! And why is this granted to me that the mother of my Lord

THERE WAS A PRIMAL HUMAN JOY IN THE MEETING OF THESE TWO EXPECTANT MOTHERS— ONE IN THE FLOWER OF YOUTH, THE OTHER'S BLOOM LONG GONE.

should come to me?" How Mary's heart must have soared. For here we see that Elizabeth recognized who Jesus really was. Here was one who immediately understood Mary's secret—that she bore the Messiah in her womb!

Elizabeth then concluded her cries with a formal beatitude. With Zechariah standing by, deaf and mute because of his unbelief, Elizabeth exclaimed, "And blessed is she who believed that there would be a fulfillment of what was spoken to her from the Lord." Inspired by the Holy Spirit, Elizabeth's words celebrated again Mary's *faith* (in contrast to Zechariah's *unbelief*) as she submitted fully to God in order to become the mother of God's Son.

W E, TOO, LIVE IN

EXPECTATION OF THE COMING

OF THE SAVIOR.

As we have moved through the account, virtually every line has added another stroke of beauty to Mary's portrait. But there is something else of immense beauty here, and that is God's care for Mary in giving her Elizabeth. Young Mary could recount Gabriel's words, but she could not be expected to fully articulate the mystery. And even if she could, who would have believed her?

But Elizabeth did! She had been prepared by her priestly husband Zechariah's dramatic experience with Gabriel, and by her own divinely wrought pregnancy. Elizabeth's profound belief in what had happened in Mary's womb—her blessing of Mary, her acknowledgment that Mary bore the Lord, her beatitude regarding Mary's faith—what a tender balm to Mary's soul! God had given young Mary a godly woman as her closest friend and confidante during this monumental time in her life.

Think of their mutuality. Both were miraculously expecting. They became sisters in experience as well as soul. Both their unborn babies had been announced by the same angel, Gabriel. Both their unborn sons had mutually fulfilling prophecies made regarding them. Imagine the women's exchange. They speculated over what the Scriptures meant. They prayed together. They talked about birth and babies. Encouragement flowed between them.

Here reality is like a dream come true. Grandmotherly Elizabeth, great with child, age lines erased by pregnancy's spring, is beside the girl-virgin. Their lives were filled with expectancy, much as it is for those who first experience the new life of Christ within.

The Visitation is flesh-and-blood history about God's care for the Virgin Mary. It is about how God directed her to a community of faith, in the humble home of Zechariah and Elizabeth, where she was linked with people of mutual belief, mutual experiences, and mutual hope.

The Visitation instructs us in the necessity of the community of faith (the church) if we are to see Christ grow in our lives. Like Mary, we must fly to the church for the encouragement of those who share a mutual faith. There we must purposely place ourselves deep within the fellowship of those who believe the same things. Like Mary, there we share the *mutual experience* of miraculous new life within. And like Mary, there our hearts are lifted up in *mutual hope and expectation.*

We, too, live in expectation of the coming of the Savior. As the apostle John so memorably explained, "Beloved, we are God's children now, and what we will be has not yet appeared; but we know that when he appears we shall be like him, because we shall see him as he is. And everyone who thus hopes in him purifies himself as he is pure" (1 John 3:2–3).

FOUR

THE MAGNIFICAT

LUKE 1:46-55

For a moment of stunning silence, Mary and Elizabeth regarded one another. And then Mary, with majestic calm, began to sing the first song of the Incarnation. Others would follow—Zechariah's song, the angels' *Gloria,* and Simeon's hymn of praise. But this song, the *Magnificat,* is the first and the greatest.

Some have wondered how so great a song—with its majestic poetry, its rich imagery, its profound theology— could have been sung by so simple a peasant girl. The *Magnificat* is indeed a brilliantly woven tapestry of Scripture, with specific parallels to the song of Hannah. Every line is an allusion to the Old Testament. But those who wonder have forgotten that every young Israelite knew by heart the great Old Testament songs of Hannah and Deborah and many Psalms of David. And could not the same Holy Spirit who overshadowed Mary at the conception of Jesus weave her words into this hallowed tapestry? The *Magnificat* was a divine/human composition, nothing less.

Lifted on the wings of the Spirit, Mary began with the unforgettable words, "My soul magnifies the Lord, and my spirit rejoices in God my Savior." Literally, the word "magnifies" means "to make great." The Latin translation is *magnificat,* from which we get the title for this great Christmas hymn.

Of course, God cannot be made any bigger. But God can be enlarged in one's life, or in one's soul, as Mary expressed it. We "magnify" God when we catch a glimpse of His greatness. He becomes all the greater in our hearts and minds when we reflect on the wonder of His creation and incarnation, on His death and atonement, on His resurrection and future return in power and glory. The deeper our understanding of His greatness, the greater our ability to "magnify" Him. Knowing that she bore the Messiah, Mary had begun to think bigger and grander thoughts than ever before.

Following her opening celebration, Mary then recited her very personal reasons for her holy magnification. Her first reason was that the Lord "has looked on the humble estate of his servant." This is a direct allusion to the humble state of barren Hannah. Like Hannah of old, Mary humbly cast herself upon God as the only one who could help.

Here we again come face to face with an essential truth of the Gospel. It is only to those who realize their need, who know that they cannot save themselves, that Christ comes. Humble, helpless Mary was a nobody from a non-place. She would give birth to Jesus on the cold earth like a stranger in her homeland.

Yet this was no accident, for such has always been God's design. Soon Jesus would begin His ministry with Isaiah's prophetic words, "The Spirit of the Lord is upon me, / because he has anointed me to proclaim good news to the poor" (Luke 4:18, quoting Isaiah 61:1). Likewise, the startling words of the Sermon on the Mount were, "Blessed are the poor in spirit, for theirs is the kingdom of heaven. Blessed are those who mourn, for they shall be comforted. Blessed are the meek, for they shall inherit the earth" (Matthew 5:3–5). The eternal truth is, "The Lord is near to the brokenhearted / and saves the crushed in spirit" (Psalm 34:18). The gift is for all who know their "humble estate"!

Mary's second reason for magnifying the Lord came in the words, "For behold, from now on all generations will call me blessed." At first glance it may seem that Mary was lifting up herself. But the focus here is not upon Mary, but upon what God is going to do for "all generations." The literal force of her statement "from now on" is that of a surprise. Mary was filled with wonder that all future generations would pronounce beatitudes over her name, until the end of the world.

The Magnificat is indeed a brilliantly woven tapestry of Scripture, with specific parallels to the Song of Hannah.

But if we are Christians—if Jesus is truly born in us—we, too, will be called blessed far beyond earth's history. Jesus Himself tells us, "Then the King will say to those on his right, 'Come, you who are blessed by my Father, inherit the kingdom prepared for you from the foundation of the world'" (Matthew 25:34). And again, "Blessed and holy is the one who shares in the first resurrection" (Revelation 20:6).

In the second half of the *Magnificat,* Mary moves from giving her *personal* reasons for magnifying the Lord to giving *prophetic* reasons. In fact, in this part of her poem Mary herself began to prophesy, using the past tense: "he has shown," "he has scattered," "he has brought down," "he has . . . exalted." If this is prophecy, we might

ask, why did Mary speak in the past tense, as if God had already accomplished all of these things? Here Mary stood in the stream of the great prophets of old. Like Isaiah and Jeremiah and Ezekiel, Mary's prophetic words were put in the past tense to emphasize two timeless truths—first, that God had indeed already done these things in past history, but also that what God will do in the future is so certain that we may properly speak of it as already having been accomplished. Thus Mary brought together history and prophecy: What God had done in the past was irrefutable evidence for what He would do in the future through the work of the Son.

What are the prophetic truths that Mary proclaimed here through the inspiration of the Holy Spirit?

First, there was the great social/moral reversal that the Messiah-Son would bring to life. Mary proclaimed that God "has scattered the proud in the thoughts of their hearts; / he has brought down the mighty from their thrones." Mary might have been looking back in history, where we see how God destroyed arrogant Pharaoh and his defiant armies; how He crushed the pride of Nebuchadnezzar, reducing him to a beast of the field until that monarch turned to God in abject humility; how He struck down Belshazzar on the very night of his strutting pride, destroying the Babylonian empire in a single day.

Most of all, though, Mary here sang of the final reversal and reckoning that awaits those who proudly reject the work of Christ. "He has scattered the proud in the thoughts of their hearts," Mary sang. Twice the New

> WHAT GOD HAD DONE IN THE PAST WAS IRREFUTABLE EVIDENCE FOR WHAT HE WOULD DO IN THE FUTURE THROUGH THE WORK OF THE SON.

Testament repeats the theme: "God opposes the proud, but gives grace to the humble" (James 4:6; 1 Peter 5:5). Those who are "proud in the thoughts of their hearts"—because of health or education or privilege or a feeling of moral superiority—are in for a rude awakening.

The Gospel lifts up the humble and casts down the proud. Life is not as it appears. Spiritually, *down is up, and up is down!* Jesus Himself is the great example. Because of His willing humiliation in the Incarnation and on the cross, He has been lifted above every power and throne. As the apostle Paul wrote,

> *Therefore God has highly exalted him and bestowed on him the name that is above every name, so that the name of Jesus every knee should bow, in heaven and on earth and under the earth, and every tongue confess that Jesus Christ is Lord, to the glory of God the Father.*
>
> PHILIPPIANS 2:9-11

GOD IS SEEKING HEARTS LIKE MARY'S— CHILDREN WHO MAGNIFY HIM IN THEIR HEARTS AND SOULS.

But Mary also sang of material/spiritual reversal: "He has filled the hungry with good things, / and the rich he has sent empty away." Here is a rock-solid principle. Those in physical/material need are typically more inclined to sense their spiritual need than are the rich and satisfied.

We can recall the rich young ruler who had everything he *thought* he needed and missed the only thing he *really* needed; or the parable of Lazarus and the rich man, who was blinded by his abundance until it was too late. Our spiritual hunger is in fact a blessed state. Paradoxically, it works like this: When we hunger spiritually, we are filled and supremely satisfied. But our satisfaction then makes way for a deeper spiritual hunger and a further filling and blessed satisfaction. And so it goes on in sublime paradox, as we become ever fuller in Christ.

This is the message of the *Magnificat*. This is the message of Christmas. Christ came to the hungry—to young Mary, to aged Simeon and Anna, to fishermen, to tax collectors, to the desperately hungry who were sent away eternally full. "Blessed are those who [continually] hunger and thirst for righteousness, for they shall be satisfied" (Matthew 5:6). The divine reward is complete satisfaction. As Jesus Himself said, "Whoever drinks of the water that I will give him will never be thirsty forever. The water that I will give him will become in him a spring of water welling up to eternal life" (John 4:14). And again, "I am the bread of life; whoever comes to me shall not hunger, and whoever believes in me shall never thirst" (John 6:35). As Mary affirmed—for the past, present, and eternal future—"He has filled the hungry with good things."

God is seeking hearts like Mary's—children who magnify Him in their hearts and souls. Theirs is the Gift of Christmas—Christ the Savior, born within—eternal life forevermore.

THE BIRTH OF JOHN

LUKE 1:56-79

Mary stayed with Elizabeth for the remaining three months of the old woman's pregnancy. Most likely she was present at the birth of John to witness this event of singular joy. Elizabeth, in the autumn of life, experienced the spring rhythm of labor and birth. And in a sublimely poignant moment, loving hands (perhaps the hands of the Virgin) placed her son into her arms. No doubt godly Elizabeth recalled the joy and laughter of another aged mother, Sarah, at the birth of Isaac. Sarah laughed, Abraham laughed, and joy filled the tents of his people. Now Elizabeth too laughed aloud and wept for joy. Zechariah laughed silently as tears coursed down his gray beard. Laughter, mixed with their son's cries, rang across the hillsides of Judea.

As Luke relates, "Her neighbors and relatives heard that the Lord had shown great mercy to her, and they rejoiced with her." At first they were incredulous; they didn't even know Elizabeth was pregnant. The secret had been well kept by mute Zechariah and the Virgin. But their initial skepticism disappeared when they came and saw for themselves radiant Elizabeth calmly nursing her son.

On the eighth day after the baby's birth, Zechariah and Elizabeth prepared for the covenant rite of circumcision. All the neighbors and relatives came in festive spirit for the happy occasion. A great crowd certainly was there; none would miss this amazing event for the firstborn of their aged friend and relative! The circumcision would mark the boy with the sign of the covenant and set him apart for the blessings promised to God's people. The fulfillment of this rite on the eighth day gave him the impeccable Jewish credentials so necessary for the Messiah's forerunner.

What was his name to be? The relatives all agreed that certainly he must be called Zechariah after his father. But immediately his mother spoke up. "No; he shall be called John." Unaware of the divinely appointed name, the relatives persisted. "They said to her, 'None of your relatives is called by this name.' And they made signs to his father, inquiring what he wanted him to be called. And he asked for a writing tablet and wrote, 'His name is John.' And they all wondered."

It is difficult for us to appreciate what a jolt this was to the family. Jewish children were *always* named after someone in the family. The double insistence of the aged couple was truly shocking. But John's divinely appointed name was intended to stir their spiritual imaginations. "John"—literally, "The Lord has given grace"—was the fitting title for the child who would be the Savior's forerunner. But there is more here, for God's choosing the child's name indicated that John's mission and power came from outside the natural order.

No sooner had Zechariah finished writing the last letter of his son's name than "immediately his mouth was opened and his tongue loosed, and he spoke, blessing God." His initial doubt had given way to faith, and faith in turn to obedience.

What a dramatic scene this was. "Fear came on all their neighbors." Luke says, "And all these things were talked about through all the hill country of Judea." Those who heard sensed that God was at work, and exhilarating fear coursed through their souls. Luke tells us that "all who heard [these things] laid them up in their hearts, saying, 'What then will this child be?' For the hand of the Lord was with him."

The night before the sunrise of Jesus' birth had, indeed, been long and bleak. According to the Scriptures the people had been living "in darkness and in the shadow of death"—like a caravan lost in a desert night, fearing for life. The faithful remnant, of course, knew that the messianic sunrise would come, for the prophet Malachi had memorably promised, "The sun of righteousness shall rise with healing in its wings. You shall go out leaping like calves from the stall" (4:2).

And now there had come the first flashes of light, prefiguring the dawn that would soon appear: Gabriel's annunciation of John to Zechariah; Gabriel's annunciation of Jesus to Mary; the meeting of the two pregnant mothers and Elizabeth's joyful prophecy; Mary's magnificent song; the birth of John the Baptist. These momentary flashes were signs assuring that the steady rays of messianic sunlight would soon shine from the horizon. Now, after the birth of John, a faint glow was almost perceptible.

His INITIAL DOUBT HAD GIVEN WAY TO FAITH, AND FAITH IN TURN TO OBEDIENCE.

Old Zechariah, nine months speechless because of unbelief, had now responded in faithful obedience. His tongue was loosed—*and he gave the final song before the sunrise.* Zechariah stood as the prophetic mouthpiece of God; his words were God's words. As with Mary's own magnificent song, his too was filled with Scripture. The hymn is traditionally called the Benedictus because the opening words—"Blessed be the Lord God of Israel"—

were rendered in the Latin Vulgate Bible with the words, "Benedictus Dominus Deus Israel." The title is fitting indeed, for this song of praise and benediction unfolded the covenant plan of God to bring salvation to the world through His coming Son.

"Zechariah," Luke records, "was filled with the Holy Spirit and prophesied":

> *"Blessed be the Lord God of Israel,*
> > *for he has visited and redeemed his people*
> *and has raised up a horn of salvation for us*
> > *in the house of his servant David,*
> *as he spoke by the mouth of his holy prophets from of old,*
> *that we should be saved from our enemies*
> > *and from the hand of all who hate us;*
> *to show the mercy promised to our fathers*
> > *and to remember his holy covenant,*
> *the oath that he swore to our father Abraham, to grant us*
> > *that we, being delivered from the hand of our enemies,*
> *might serve him without fear,*
> > *in holiness and righteousness before him all our days."*

*T*HIS SONG

BEFORE THE SUNRISE

WAS AN ECSTATIC CHAIN

OF PRAISE FROM

BEGINNING TO END.

This song before the sunrise was an ecstatic chain of praise from beginning to end. In this first half Zechariah recounted God's eternal covenants to David and Abraham. The immediate context of God's promise to David was that Solomon would succeed him on the throne. But the final fulfillment was to come in the future, when God would place His own Son on the Davidic throne to rule over His eternal Kingdom forever. The mighty "horn of salvation" is the King of kings and Lord of lords who redeems us and delivers us from our sins.

Today this mighty "horn of salvation" is able "to save to the uttermost those who draw near to God through him" (Hebrews 7:25). Whoever we are, whatever we have done, no matter how heinous our sin—whether it is murder, infidelity, perversion, betrayal, embezzlement, lying, jealousy, hateful gossip, or whatever—Christ, the "horn of salvation," can save us completely and eternally. This is the wonder of the Gospel—"it is the power of God for salvation to everyone who believes" (Romans 1:16).

Similarly, Zechariah hearkened back even further to God's covenant promise to Abraham. As the apostle Paul wrote, Abraham "'believed God, and it was counted to him as righteousness' . . . [and] it is those of faith who are the sons of Abraham" (Galatians 3:6–7). Moreover, "If [we] are Christ's, then [we] are Abraham's offspring, heirs according to promise" (3:29).

As Zechariah came to the middle of his song, we can well imagine that his eyes fell to his newborn son, and he sang of his part in the new day:

> *"And you, child, will be called the prophet of the Most High;*
> *for you will go before the Lord to prepare his ways,*
> *to give knowledge of salvation to his people*
> *in the forgiveness of their sins."*

What incredible things Zechariah sang regarding his son! True "knowledge of salvation" and "the forgiveness of sins" would come from his ministry. This is what the Gospel offers: authentic forgiveness—the only real forgiveness of sins in the universe. Those who have experienced it can testify that there is nothing like it. It is complete and penetrates to the depth of our being.

Zechariah ended his song with praise for the imminent rising of the Sun:

> "... *because of the tender mercy of our God*
>   *whereby the sunrise shall visit us from on high*
> *to give light to those who sit in darkness and in the shadow of death,*
> *to guide our feet into the way of peace."*

Here was the fulfillment of Malachi's prophecy: "But for you who fear my name, the sun of righteousness shall rise with healing in its wings. You shall go out leaping like calves from the stall" (4:2). Jesus is "the morning star" who rises in our hearts (2 Peter 1:19). He is "the root and the descendant of David, the bright morning star" (Revelation 22:16). Of Himself Jesus said, "I am the light of the world. Whoever follows me will not walk in darkness, but will have the light of life" (John 8:12).

When Jesus rises in our lives, gone is "the shadow of death." We pass from death to life. He guides "our feet into the way of peace." He gives His promise, "Peace I leave with you; my peace I give to you" (John 14:27). And we "leap like calves released from the stall"—heels in the air, free and complete!

THIS IS THE WONDER OF THE GOSPEL—"IT IS THE POWER OF GOD FOR SALVATION TO EVERYONE WHO BELIEVES."

SIX

THE BIRTH OF CHRIST

LUKE 2:1–20

From ground level, Joseph and Mary were insignificant nobodies from a nothing town. They were peasants. They were poor, uneducated, of no account.

Joseph and Mary capsulized the mystery of grace—because the King does not come to the proud and powerful, but to the poor and powerless. As happens so often in life, things were not as they seemed to the world around, because humble Mary and Joseph were the father and mother of the King of kings.

They appeared to be helpless pawns caught in the movements of secular history. But every move was being made by the hand of God. The Messiah *had* to be born in tiny, insignificant Bethlehem! As the virgin traveled, she bore under her steady beating heart, hidden from the world, the busy thumping heart of God.

The baby Mary carried was not a Caesar, a man who would claim to be a god, but a far greater wonder—God who had become a man!

We are all familiar with the haunting simplicity of Luke's description of the birth: "While they were there, the time came for her to give birth. And she gave birth to her firsborn son."

In Bethlehem, the accommodations for travelers were primitive. The eastern inn was the crudest of arrangements. Typically it was a series of stalls built on the inside of an enclosure and opening onto the common yard where the animals were kept. All the innkeeper provided was fodder for the animals and a fire to cook on. On that cold day when the expectant parents arrived, nothing at all was available, not even one of those crude stalls. And despite the urgency, no one would make room for them. So it was probably in the common courtyard where the travelers' animals were tethered that Mary gave birth to Jesus—with only Joseph attending.

If we imagine that it was into a freshly swept County Fair stable that Jesus was born, we miss the whole point. It was wretched—scandalous! There was sweat and pain and blood and cries as Mary reached to the stars for help. The earth was cold and hard. The smell of birth was mixed into a wretched bouquet with the stench of manure and acrid straw. Trembling carpenter's hands, clumsy with fear, grasped God's Son slippery with blood—the baby's limbs waving helplessly as if falling through space—his face grimacing as he gasped the cold and his cry pierced the night.

It was a leap down—as if the Son of God rose from his splendor, stood poised at the rim of the universe, and dove headlong, speeding through the stars over the Milky Way to earth's galaxy, finally past Arcturus, where he plunged into the virgin's womb where he was carried until birth in the midst of a huddle of animals. Nothing could be lower.

Luke finishes the picture: Mary "wrapped him in swaddling cloths and laid him in a manger, because there was no place for them in the inn." Mary counted his fingers. She and Joseph wiped him clean as best they could by firelight, and Mary wrapped each of his little round, steaming arms and legs with strips of cloth—mummy-like. No one helped her. She laid him in a feeding trough.

No child born into the world that day seemed to have lower prospects. The Son of God was born into the world not as a prince but as a pauper. We must never forget that this is where Christianity began—and where it always begins. It begins with a sense of need, a graced sense of one's insufficiency. Christ comes to the needy. Ultimately he is born in those who are "poor in spirit."

The story moves quickly as Christ's birth is announced. Shepherds were the first to hear. "And in the same region there were shepherds out in the field, keeping watch over their flock by night. And an angel of the Lord appeared to them, and the glory of the Lord shone around them, and they were filled with fear." The shepherds on that wintry night were naturally huddled close to their fire, while above, the icy constellations swept by. Suddenly, as if a star burst, glory dazzled the night, and an honored angel stepped forth as the shepherds recoiled in great fear—despite his reassuring words.

That the message came to shepherds first, and not to the high and mighty, once again brings us to the refrain that God comes to the needy, the "poor in spirit." Shepherds were despised by the "good," respectable people of that day. They were regarded as thieves. The only ones lower than shepherds at this particular time in Jewish history were lepers.

God wants us to get it straight: He comes to those who sense their need. He does not come to the self-sufficient. Christmas is for those who need Jesus! Whatever our situation, He can deliver us. The angel said the "good news" was for "all the people." Whoever you are, He can deliver you. As the writer of the epistle of Hebrews puts it, Christ "is able to save to the uttermost those who draw near to God through him, since he always lives to make intercession for them" (Hebrews 7:25). Listen to the angel's words again, slowly: "Fear not, for behold, I bring you good news of a great joy that will be for all the people. For unto you is born this day in the city of David a Savior, who is Christ the Lord."

Now see what happens.

"And suddenly there was with the angel a multitude of the heavenly host praising God and saying,
"Glory to God in the highest,
and on earth peace among those with whom he is pleased!"

Here we need a little Christmas imagination. Perhaps there was a flash, and suddenly the bewildered shepherds were surrounded by angels.

The angels departed, the glory that lit the countryside faded, the constellations reappeared, and the shepherds were alone. They allowed no grass to grow under their feet. They took off running, leaping the low Judean fences, and entered the enclosure wide-eyed and panting. They searched the stalls and quickly found the new mother and her Babe out in the open among the animals. Immediately they began to announce the good news, telling all who would listen about the angels and the baby. When they left, they continued glorifying and praising God for all they had experienced.

This Christmas it is not enough to hear about Jesus. It is not enough to come peek in the manger and say, "Oh, how nice. What a lovely scene. It gives me such good feelings." The truth is, if Christ were born in Bethlehem a thousand times but not in you, you would be eternally lost. The Christ who was born into the world must be born in your heart.

Christmas sentiment without the living Christ is a yellow brick road to darkness. That is the terrifying thing about all the Christmas glitz—that Christmas can be buried by materialism, and sentiment and people will not even know it or care.

He really did come into the world; and because of this, He really can come into your heart. This Christmas, let us lay our lives before Him and receive the gift.

SEVEN

THE PRESENTATION

I t had been forty days since Mary felt the pains of birth and first held her little Son against her breast. Now Joseph and Mary had just finished retracing their journey, this time traveling as three to Jerusalem. But why would they travel again so soon and with their little one not yet six weeks old? As Dr. Luke explains:

> And when the time came for their purification according to the Law of Moses, they brought him up to
> Jerusalem to present him to the Lord (as it is written in the Law of the Lord, "Every male who first opens
> the womb shall be called holy to the Lord") and to offer a sacrifice according to what is said in the Law
> of the Lord.

Luke's words are pregnant with meaning. Here the Giver of the Law is fulfilling the Law. Here is the newborn Son being presented to the Father whose loving embrace He had known for all eternity. Here is a sacrifice being offered for the One who would Himself become the sacrifice for all the world.

How Joseph and Mary must have retraced their memories as they retraced their steps that day on the way to Jerusalem. Was there still a hint of fear as Mary recalled Gabriel's astounding words?—"Do not be afraid, Mary, for you have found favor with God. And behold, you will conceive in your womb and bear a son."

Their child was to be called "Jesus"—literally, "Jehovah is salvation."

Surely the wonder of the recent weeks burned bright in their thoughts and words as they made their way to Jerusalem—how the skies had blazed with a myriad of angels; how the shepherds had run, leaping the low pasture fences, shouting the news, "The Savior has been born!"

As they reflected on those days since the first light of Christmas morn, surely they returned often to their little Son's name. "You shall call his name Jesus," Gabriel had announced to Mary. And Gabriel repeated the identical words to Joseph, "You shall call his name Jesus" (Matthew 1:21). And so it was, as Luke records, that "at the end of eight days, when he was circumcised, he was called Jesus."

It was important that Christ be circumcised. Circumcision was commanded for all males who would be a part of Abraham's household. Without it He would not be identified with His people, even though he was of pure Hebrew blood.

But the matter of greatest significance was his name—Jesus—officially given at His circumcision. Certainly Mary and Joseph had often discussed His name, both before His birth and during the weeks that followed. But when the time for circumcision came and Joseph uttered the divinely given name, the sense of the moment must have overwhelmed them. Their child was to be called "Jesus"—literally, "Jehovah is salvation."

With the Temple towering before them, how small Mary and Joseph must have felt approaching the altar to offer their sacrifice, "a pair of turtledoves, or two young pigeons." It was a poor woman's offering. We know this because the book of Leviticus requires a yearling lamb—except, as Moses wrote, "If she cannot afford a lamb, then she shall take two turtledoves or two pigeons, one for a burnt offering and the other for a sin offering" (12:8). The humble bird-offering of Mary and Joseph was a public declaration of their poverty. And so we are reminded again— it is the persistent refrain of Christ's birth—that God does not come to the self-sufficient, but to those of humble state who hunger and thirst for the gift of the Savior.

But before Mary and Joseph could even approach the altar, they themselves were approached by a man with outstretched arms, his face radiant with joy and expectation. What a welcome they must have received! The words of Scripture tell it best:

> Now there was a man in Jerusalem, whose name was
> Simeon, and this man was rightous and devout, waiting

for the consolation of Israel, and the Holy Spirit was upon him. And it had been revealed to him by the Holy Spirit that he would not see death before he had seen the Lord's Christ. And he came in the Spirit into the temple, and when the parents brought in the child Jesus, to do for him according to the custom of the Law, he took him up in his arms and blessed God.

Here is something more to put in our treasury of Christmas memories. We see the stooped profile of Simeon, advanced in years, with age-spotted hands but a soul that was brimming with life! "Righteous and devout," Simeon knew that the only hope was the mercy and grace of God. He longed for righteousness; he thirsted for consolation. How long had he been waiting? Days? Months? Years? We cannot know. But we can imagine his quiet assurance as daily he came to the Temple looking. "Is this the one? There's a likely couple! Maybe this is Him!"

And then on that great day, the Holy Spirit prompted him. Moved by the Spirit, Simeon accosted Mary and Joseph—and with trembling arms lifted the fat, dimpled baby from the startled virgin. And for a moment the world ceased to turn as he received God Incarnate into his quaking hands. He looked at Jesus . . . and looked . . . and looked again. And his heart soared in prophetic song:

> *"Lord, now you are letting your servant depart in peace,*
> *according to your word;*

WITH THE BABY IN HIS ARMS, IN THE AURA OF GOD'S PRESENCE, SIMEON EXPERIENCED A PROFOUND SOUL-PEACE.

for my eyes have seen your salvation

      that you prepared in the presence of all peoples,

a light for revelation to the Gentiles,

      and for glory to your people Israel."

With the baby in his arms, in the aura of God's presence, Simeon experienced a profound soul-peace. And well he should, for he held the "Prince of Peace." "The sun of righteousness" had come; the day of redemption had dawned. With his own eyes Simeon had seen the salvation of the Lord.

Do we see the amazing significance of this moment? It was not lost on Joseph and Mary, for the child's "father and . . . mother marveled at what was said about him." May we too come to profound amazement—and thus hold every word close to our heart.

But from the lofty heights of ecstasy, Simeon quickly brings us back to the reality of our need for the Savior and what the work of our salvation would mean. "This child is appointed," Simeon proclaims, "for the fall and rising of many in Israel, and for a sign that is opposed . . . so that thoughts from many hearts may be revealed."

"For the fall and rising"—unwelcome though these words sound to the world today, again we hear the persistent theme of Christmas. For only when we fall before the Savior in humiliation and poverty of spirit will we rise to new life in Christ. What a message of hope! For the grace of humility, unlike riches or power, is available to all. "The Lord is near to the brokenhearted and saves the crushed in spirit," the psalmist says (34:18). Like Mary, we can rejoice in our "humble estate," for Christ comes to us in our greatest need.

But what of Simeon's closing words? "A sword will pierce through your own soul also." Mary would indeed know the blessedness of the *Magnificat,* but she would also know the sorrow foretold by Simeon. There would be the flight into Egypt. Her Son would be despised and rejected. There would be His passion. A sword would pierce the Savior's side as He bore the sins of the world on the cross. But a sword would also pierce His mother's soul. How costly was the Gift God gave. How great His love for us. "For God so loved the world, that he gave his only Son, that whoever believes in him should not perish but have eternal life" (John 3:16).

As we too retrace the memories of that first Christmas, we discover anew the "sun of righteousness" who comes "with healing in [His] wings." What a plunging leap He took—as if the Son of God rose from His heavenly splendor, stood poised on the rim of the universe, and dove headlong through the galaxies to be born of a simple peasant girl in a crude and humble place. But here we see the wonder of Christmas! The Gift comes only to those who humbly know their need, "who hunger and thirst for righteousness."

To all who will He promises, "I am the resurrection and the life. Whoever believes in me, though he die, yet shall he live; and everyone who lives and believes in me shall never die" (John 11:25–26).

Here is the Gift of Christmas—

Christ the Savior born in our hearts—

eternal life forevermore.

I am the resurrection and the life.

Whoever believes in me, though he die,

yet shall he live; and everyone who lives

and believes in me shall never die.

JOHN 11:25—26